D0861332

EASTER

Poems by David Craig

EASTER

Poems by David Craig

Angelico Press

First published in the USA
by Angelico Press
© David Craig 2022

For information, address:
Angelico Press
169 Monitor St.
Brooklyn, NY 11222
www.angelicopress.com

pbk: 978-1-62138-835-7
cloth: 978-1-62138-836-4

Cover Design: Michael Schrauzer
Cover Image: Linda Craig,
Master and Disciple, 2022, mixed media

Thanks to Linda, my life,
and to Fr. Gregory Hyde, S.J.

TABLE OF CONTENTS

No Man Can Create This
—covid

Snow, like our quasi-plague, begins melting;
though nothing's in bloom: running sidewalk water
is the only sign of life. Still, people feel cheer—

spring has begun to have its say, to open
its huge creaking medieval doors. You can hear them,
allowing the world another day. (The Apocalypse

can, for a while, take a nap beneath a tree.)
So I do my part—don't pick the first flower I see.
I want to allow the dance to begin. Let our irises,

a host of purple kingdoms, offer what comes.
Though my youth continues its wane, my wife still bandies
her art. That's how the Holy Ghost shouts

the Father's name: in paintings, pianos, left-overs.
Just this morning, in fact, I heard my first robin, outside
the main classroom building, in the ruined choir of a tree,

the whole of creation, designed and singing just for me!
He's a Voice that helps to invent us, in droplets of snow.
No man can create this, no man may take it away.

I

Stone-Look Field Tile

When we stroll out into the fine night of our sins,
there's no coaxing involved: our manse, comfort—conspires;
our ostentation is subtle, a touch of split roughage

in the ceiling beams. We pay for every satisfaction.
(A large lake, a dock behind.) Fresh company always
seems to be in the summer offing. But who

can fool the self when every lake is a fiction?
You know very well where you're not standing: on porcelain
stone-look field tile. It would be a nice walk, but to where? . . .

So goes our sense of self; nothing there that money
can't buy. A place where we might right each dismay.
Each foray, misdirected! We'll be what's left when Jesus

has finished with us, nothing the moment before!
We need the disappointing tally. Jesus, give us
what we need—then give us that again. We live

among ruins. We speak best under charred timber.
Our voices scarred by moonlight, gin rummy in the kitchen.
Everything we've owned has passed—before we got here.

After a Storm

Bless the beach, the bundled sea. Bless the reach
that almost takes us there. We always sing best
when what we want is beyond our grasp. This is

the only way we can possess the days.
It frees us. That's why I can take my Down's guy
for a spin so often in the car. The bar is low—

but the sky is not. On some days the clouds, the trees,
just open up. It's a welcome collusion, the voices
of leaves and wind, God on the back roads.

Then we come home, with Jesus, to our back door
at dusk (having walked over the pleasant green grass);
we end our days playing Uno-Flip on a table.

Way past our bedtimes, my wife and I are no worse
for the earthly wear. The house soon joins us, settles
down. We find our pillows as we talk—cataloguing

His hand. We wish for nothing. Sleep is the balm
for that. I don't know if fairies attend us, or if
an angel sings Bach's Mass in the middle of the street.

He Sits like Krishna

He is so quiet when He doesn't come, His place,
chairs, empty: scattered newspapers, a pet hamster
running on a mythical wheel. Then He chooses, brings

morning. It's really just that simple; He sits
in your sunny rooms like Krishna, little bells, ringing
in His hands. Don't ask Him to explain; He hasn't time.

He's going to a bonfire tonight with fast foreign cars,
the Coen brothers. He's busy, opens His pen
by holding the cap in His mouth while talking, giving

three directions at once. He had time for Milton. He has time
for you. He's the great Ear of the universe, pierced
in the breeze. (He has friends in SoHo.) Don't expect what you

expect! That's a place to start. Whatever happens can build—
or move by like a river. Either way, it shouldn't
make much difference to you. We're the children here,

at the crossroads, so many directions in front of us,
each like a land we'll never visit. (Many
of those are real!) Each port is a kind of home.

Son and Grandson, Hand in Hand, Next to the Garage

It's a quiet fold, Mary's, a sunny day
for my son and grandson as they begin to walk
away from us, next to the garage's wildflowers.

We won't have to be here at the end to know that the Spirit
has made life good. (Whose heart in this house doesn't fly
with that little boy's joys? His moods, reactions, surely

have become our own.) We'll work the ropes and shutters,
our ship over neighborhood seas. "Come along, little captain,"
I'll say when he's older if I get the chance. "We've cannons

to the left of us, and stumps for our legs. We'll take
enough of this island to give us a bounty or two."
Mary will be out back with Linda, hanging

the day on the line. The world is their housecoat. (Laughter
rises with the frame drum and a horse-hide mallet.)
You never have to go far! "Joseph," the future

says. We'll watch, no matter where we'll be!
And when he becomes a man, my son, older,
we, in heaven, will see them completed—and the next.

Van Gogh's Prostate

I want stars, their sharp golden edges testing my palms;
I want a high sparkling wire to walk on inside me.
How else will I know myself? Or train my feet?

Van Gogh, a funambulist, would have it no other way.
Excess helped him to see the French countryside, to know
the real color and feel of straw. God always

finds us in fields, like today—unfit, not ready.
(We're like the world's oldest baking apprentices.
And who could blame us: the puffed bread when it

comes out of the French oven, its smell kills us!
It doesn't matter if the world takes better roads.
We'll still meet on Tuesdays, sponsor a little league team.

We'll hang its picture at the local Pizza Hut.
No one will find the real us, no one has ever
been able to—because we run at night,

flapping under hides, sharpening the crescent. We stop
for nothing—until mornings come.) I'll be someone
else you greet after Mass on Sunday afternoon.

The Mucous Snails Leave in Washington State
—for Leonard Koscianski

We can recognize sin by the mucous it leaves on the forest
floor, and grace by the ways it effects our skin:
soft rains, a haze of sun, the way our bare feet

engage the damp earth, carefully, one step at a time.
Last year's humus takes up next year's cause.
And whose heart does not go after the fallen red leaves,

each with its important say? We spend most of our time
between the two, humbling along, collecting fuel
for our fires. Beauty sustains us—because it hurts.

We can't treasure everything that passes, but time
does its work. Human flowers reach to the extent
they plumb. That's why St. Francis always talked about hell.

We are all just one move away. Leaves and fruits,
the payoffs, require more water, and so rot faster
than the humbler root and stem. The coarser our garment,

the better our handshake, the closer we are to sin.
It's a better fit, that world—though it seems medieval.
(Since it comes with a scooter, I sign on the dotted line.)

Nomadland, West Virginia
—for Jack-Attack, my neighbor

So much work to be done, so little time!
I'll be holding up my loose, beltless pants with one hand
at heaven's gate, keeping my shirt together

with the other. St. Peter will understand, another dusty
roadling who wants to lift his place on the run.
They'll be old time-y prairie schooners there, broken

axles, kids from across the street, their faces
smiling out of ripped canvass. (How'd they get so tall?)
Then you'll see you didn't necessarily do everything wrong;

you were just possessed of a different kind of right,
part of Jesus's collection: a panoply of relatively
hard-working trailer riffraff, one-handed friends.

Heaven's a place where you can razz your neighbors.
Jack, mine, made a standing offer, "The keys are in the truck."
(I was hauling slag, trying to put in a backyard.)

He's gone now, Parkinson's. His wife moved them south
to be closer to their grown children. All the hard work's
been done. It's too late to pull the petals off that rose.

The Sloth Poem

Two-toed, sloths move slowly, defecate once
a week. (Half of them die during this vulnerable time.)
I mention this because it helps get us slowly to us.

Spiritually, I'm a distant relative of his—though no one
has had the energy to check this out. (Sloths do
not have genealogy societies, and their libraries are scant.)

Still, I'm no Francis, or even a Leo (the slow),
and St. Therese is a 747 who flies by so fast
that she fluffs the hair on my turning furry head.

Nope. Nope again. Each sloth must accept himself.
His place farther back in the pack. No one even notices
when he stops to pull out a cigarette, begin his smoke.

This somehow suits him. (It takes him two minutes to scratch
an ear.) And his voice doesn't help. It never catches
its prey. He's not a bad guy. Actually people like him

once they get to know him. (That takes about a year.)
Once he makes a friend, however, he has one for life—
in part because the other has fallen so far behind.

The Movie *Nomadland*

Is it true that destitution alone makes for community?
Is it true that when you've got nothing, you can finally give—
maybe a beat-up old car seat near Tucson, Arizona?

This is how love always comes: limping, maybe missing
a few teeth. It comes in a van, if that's your home.
It comes when you spit after brushing into desert scrub.

Money always separates—and perhaps that's why
it must go. What are the endgame economics of love?
The hand that reaches from need to the nearest need.

This is, after all, how God comes. Spent, mutilated.
Lord, give us poverty before we die in our greed,
surrounded by little fences. Death shrinks us until

we become as clean as a welcome desert wind,
as the next person who wears suffering with her smile.
Jesus lives there. After all, we make each other,

are the only things that can—in our errors, returns.
"You can use my hedge clippers. They're rusty, but that
will build up your arms." "We'll call it an arms race!"

A Glass of Chilled Champagne

Spring continues to slowly open—us;
and before you know it, students are sitting outside,
while my new colleague—not teaching—walks up the campus

hill in shorts, sport coat and sunglasses. The veil
between this life and the next has, for the moment,
gotten thinner. The future eases every flower

out of its glove; greener grass gives the world
a better face. And we, happy as gulls
on a trash heap, don't even care about what's next.

The trees expand to speak their piece, and the end-times
must wait a little; though by tomorrow, snow
might be piled again on the bushes. The seasons proceed

without us, don't they? A demonstration, as if God were
    showing
us His fiddle, how He plays time itself. You have
to attend to catch the spreading of leafy fingers.

He continues with this all through the summer, and then
it's red leaves falling again. We spiral to prayer.
Winter soon sings, a glass of chilled champagne.

Rilke's Letter to My Students

My students ask how long will this project take?
The rest of their lives! That's why we're on this train.
There's no use pretending we can walk in perfect ease.

Everything's metaphor because nothing is. We're the thing
half-finished, a lasting tribute to our Maker. May He
complete us finally, half-saints, and close the deal.

Ulysses S. Grant knew this when he threw more troops
at death. It's why he gave back his lunch. It's why
he donated too much of himself to drink. (Who can know

the arc of generals?) There is no bow in Christendom.
We have to give what we haven't completely gathered.
Can't ever, not here. There is no other way.

We can only offer our bodies in battle—for Love.
This project's about Him. For though your youth will take
you far—it won't be far enough. (The last page

will come for you!) That's why the churches in Europe
are dark and cool. It's you who must bring the heat.
Think of it: a tall lean of all those lit candles!

Aquinas on Rats

If rats run in western packs, does their alpha sport
a moustache? Does he have a dusty cowboy hat
he can slap to his thigh when he needs a little mayhem?

You can see his scarred nose twitch in the rat saloon,
and you know where the scene is going, to small boot hill.
(A group is called a "mischief"; some live in trees.)

I suppose they'd have their own rules, after natural law.
The women probably show out, most neatly attired.
They'd have art, culture, love to work in wire and wood.

And though a rat will never be elected president,
nor will he be consulted by the Harvard school of law,
he can mate and eat, my brother; he's mastered the essentials!

We're like that, in a way, though some of us are too old
to be chasing pinkies. Still, he sings for me.
We each want our place, every blessed rat in the universe.

He weeps sometimes in open fields, into his little
cup of beer. Too many rats in his hole, a foot
in his face. He needs Jesus—an epic, a resolution.

In the Middle of Nowhere

I want to be a voice I've never heard,
an unanswered prayer—a morning that never completely
comes. I want to build my home there, to watch

the clouds when I please. Nothing has to happen.
The place will be its own answer. The call of God.
(Unobtrusive, you will spot it by the flowerbeds: simple,

spare, though the colors will speak.) There might be a fence,
plain shutters and brick, a bay window. The house will be small.
It will not be unlike the one you already know.

Rosaries fit easily into small hands. When horizons
stretch out so, in every direction, this is what you'll get!
(Such are the petals of heaven.) The sheriff's car

might be parked out in front of it, but that just means
a box of donuts, with sprinkles, on the kitchen table.
After all these years, you still like the sound of his keys!

Such order is beyond you. But steps can be negotiated.
What life is not a matter of give and die?
In what game do you hold all the cards?

Lenten Fail

Sheep, quick victims, must learn to sleep lightly.
I, on the other hand, slow-wave it through Lent.
My reach has faded again—as Easter opens

the year. I'm finished before I'm quite through; though
    everyone,
if pressed, would certainly admit that the sunrise this morning
was strikingly beautiful. Birds and flowers still carry on

as if nothing much has changed—and in truth it hasn't;
though this is not to say that our actions completely
indict us. No, it just means that this is how

we annually lose in Lent: we settle down
into ourselves like sacks of purchased flour
on a buckboard. For weeks we stood tall in the store!

Such is a father's love—one healthy scrub
in the tub, and the child's clean again. Free to go
about his business, to laugh as he's always done,

beneath the too busy eye of the world. Let each person's
laughter define him! How else can our failures complete us,
except under an early sun—its perpetual refutation?

A Mile is Now Two

Christ is Risen. And so the earth itself
has expanded. A mile is now two. Old Testament prophets
have set up impromptu stalls at the West Side Market.

(You don't have to turn the pages!) The butchers aren't giving
the meat away, but they're making lots of new friends.
For some this is a bit much, so goodness also goes

underground, in each handshake. (This allows a place
for everyone, an easier commerce.) Some only need
one morning—then nothing is ever the same. You might think

this is heaven, and you'd be right: the sunny wave
that tides us, the one thought which gives life to the others.
You'll also find quiet here, scampering squirrels;

your voice like October, when the leaves start to redden,
    tumble.
There'll be fewer people around, but one word goes farther
there, each gesture endures. Whoever shows up

is welcome, because he has earned his name. It's the season
for Jesus and hot soup. Mary sews on the porch.
Each creak in her rocker brings us quilts, the tides.

Jesuit Retreat House and a Most Delicate Impulse, Ignored

We work the territories of time, where Love snatches flies
with a Pecos tongue, where answers emerge like lizards,
squinting in the cowboy dust. If this were a Western,

we'd lower the brim of our hats—still get it wrong.
Distracted directors, we'd miss the sound of bees:
their antennae, jointed; the Ohio flowers, their motion

in the wind. When Jesus rose up, we started to.
But we've never completed the act. (Thankfully, even hell
has this door!) Joy is the pulse that saves us. It encourages

us with what we know. Life calls itself names.
Ours! Come—under Retreat House trees. The deer
come close. The sun partners with living nature,

creates dramas in the high and contrary seaward
movement of tree limbs, leaves. In the varied distances,
the sunshine, different species deliver the dance.

I rosaried it twice, most of me forgetting about Mass—
religion defeating itself! My director queried.
I shrugged, some part of me had chosen the lesser.

The Myth of the Easter King

The Easter king rowed his way here from Europe.
An exile, he rules a demesne of questionable ideas,
has set up a kind of immigrant-friendly underground

using sewing machines. He owns half of Newark;
he's steady when it comes to business, ignores the fads,
the flair of McDonald's, the brutality of football.

He ignores the work ethic too, the Rotary—though he still
has one of those phones. He pours his liquor into little
old glasses, sometimes thinks of moving his operation

to Utah. But he's built a life on separating fact
from fiction—though he likes a fireplace as much as anyone.
He prefers old ways, the thing cleanly given, the squared-off

corner. His place is in the background. His quiet
skills go unnoticed. He abides for centuries at a time,
making new friends, sometimes packing musty bags.

(The bunny is always sending him invitations.) If he sees
you a second time, the glasses come out. He sparkles,
offers. You'll be expected to pour, to speak your mind.

Easter Lilies

—a sunny verb—in every empty fountain.
That's why I like most mornings. This cast finds hope
in a company of weeds, in strawberry breakfast toast.

I hurry to shop for a Cavs hoodie. It's cold
in this retreat house basement. I try my joy
in Walmart, bless the cashier, though we don't talk much.

I hum Your name in the parking lot, get back
to my quiet. Our lives are so small sometimes, almost
silly—that Old English word meaning "blessed"; a behavior

odd enough to lose its meaning. Catherine Doherty
engraved Francis on her cabin in the Canadian woods:
"The Lord has asked me to be a fool the likes

of which the world has never seen." Urodivoi—
not such a jump for most of us. A sepulcher
designed to wake you up, dead, pilgrim. You're the dance

in the bright trees again today, a call
from the One who owns us, in a mass of boughs wagging.
At that point, we're everything nobody gets to see.

Easter, Retreat's End

Easter buoys. It keeps showing up in our efforts.
The last thing you get in this season is sustained peace.
Think of the rose, how it grows, perplexing itself

at every turn. Its colors astound the poor creature.
Its reach redefines its grasp. Despite this, it knows
its every attribute is a prayer that answers prayer.

We can sit next to one, bob with the breeze,
the fire-thorn stems. And when we get up and leave,
that good is gone: a part of the earth, our future

friends. The slow wet road sounds—what we have
to give. You can hear it under trees: my youth.
(These good Jesuits who absorbed my high school unruliness.)

When I get back home I'll be a tinker again,
on my bridge, hawking my wears. I'll sell my goods
because life is only full when I pass it along.

Each stranger's face is a glimpse of what I need—
a chance to enter their hearts, a call to hear
(though it echoes best outside, among the trees.)

On the Look of His Walking Back
—Retreat House

Trees down in the forest, branches blocking the path;
the good days come so naturally after rain.
Not that any of it matters. Your feet crunch the pebbles—

a barn door still opens somewhere. New life begins
to stir. This is called Easter. It's much larger
than you. It's like you're walking inside a great ear

out of doors—most leaves high up waft like a distant
sea in these trees, seahorses. I open order's
mouth when I open mine. Answers come

because they have never left us. May we be part
of that, the small-town residue which makes up for so much
that's missing: Our Lady as she fishes, barefoot, off a pier.

You just have to be yourself. I felt at home in the woods
today, when a buck on the deepest path wouldn't let
me pass. My smallest joy, defeated! I had

to rearrange my narrative, my hope. God forward,
and on the look of His walking back. We find
our way to a new self, a diminished joy.

The Future will be Chinese

We'll have a finished quality, without the glide
preparation affords. (Praise be to Whom it belongs.)
It's an Easter thing. Our mistaken pasts, forsworn.

(Those hands will have gotten what they were reaching for—
nothing.) Our days will become what they've always been.
Squirrels will miter freedom. Everything will be

startlingly new, like today, which hurt itself
when it opened. (I know. I was there.) We owe everything to
a completion which will happen, because it already moves us.

We don't need to watch as this world creates itself
through cracks in our broken neighborhood sidewalks. Asphalt
could never stem this childlike tide. This sea

will continue for as long as we barefoot this grass. Think
of the picnics! Children marching down bannered streets!
The new will surely outflank us, distress our understanding.

In the end we will have to give over to it. We won't
be calling our shots. Our childhood idols will reappear
in unfamiliar clothes. The future will be Chinese.

When Jesus (and Gainsborough) Rises

A quaking bird at your feet: this is what you remember.
You were seldom a child yelling with the others—you walked
around lost, the kid dressed in painterly blue.

Almost a Gainsborough! How could you be expected to
    proceed?
(Fit only for a portrait.) Or was that what you felt on the inside?
Was this what God had intended, that over-arching

Someone who owned the pews, the only sense
available back then? Years later the boy took to drink!
Each person, they say, acts his message out.

How else could we matter? And no one regrets, in the end,
what he's gone through. It hardly seems worth the notice.
Everyone has the same climb. We could've been born

in Yonkers, our dad, a barber. (I'd like to thank all
of you gathered here!) This is how we proceed: one eminently
forgettable story after another, a spiritual

version of manifest destiny. We look out, and the war
is over. Easter rises, as it always has:
a bird might come to your hand—or grandchildren to your
    feet!

This Land, and Woody Guthrie
—for a student whose dad read James Whitcomb Riley to her when she was a child

Our sins are like little clams inside, always yapping.
You'd think they would learn the flamenco. And I don't help,
with my regressions. How hard it must be to be Pope!

Each word has to be crafted, shaved, without losing the form
that gave it rise. Each a carved little wooden soldier.
He needs to make them march. Each new one new.

When I open my mouth, too, leaves should move,
birds alight. I would know their names. You would find us
     nesting
with herons, in the cannon's mouth. Small towns in America

would finally happen. No kid would ever play Superman
again. You could buy jams for half the price.
Cows would saunter down Main, Holy Water next

to drinking fountains. (Out west, too, Woody could embrace
the distances. He'd baptize Cheyenne's railroad yards.)
In Greenfield, Indiana, you'd see a bluer sky.

We'd know about silo work, how to set type.
Angels would visit more often, or feel free enough
to materialize: for birthday parties, swimming holes.

Under Neo-Gothic Construction

Who knew what to expect once that stone rolled away?
We're suddenly talking about commerce, large cabasas,
my beaded sombrero. Friends have appeared everywhere.

There's just no stopping the laughter, the goings-on
at the smallest cafeteria tables. Anyone who wants in
gets room, a free packaged game of jarts.

The music is exactly what you would have chosen. Saints
walk casually among us, are happy to work the barbie.
Things you say suddenly take import; it's like

the grass is listening. Rocks are your oldest friends.
(Sometimes we have to wait for the rest of the world
to catch up!) In the meantime we'll make movies, begin

to build Gaudi's La Pedrera in Weirton, West Virginia.
How, I ask you, can we repay the lark?
Who could teach the otter to swim? Mary delights

in heavenly meadows—all of them. Which of our ends
has ever transpired? Can we even speak for the rest
of the day: a blossom in a little too much wind?

On Hearing Too Late
—a prayer for "Sorrows"

Old friend, a flame, she passed before I knew it—
along with everything I didn't give. What repentance
could be vast enough to cover what I could not?

Nothing glib will help here. Could I have kept up?
Maybe. She was an old friend's wife, though, a guy
who'd cut himself off. How vast mercy has to be!

I've been a bargain for no one, even as I've aged.
How different from my heroes, who've blessed us all as we've
    passed
in a line beneath them, each one under a hand.

Is there anyone here who hasn't been a self-satisfied
fool? Delores, bless you and your husband, Craig.
I hope you had a batch of kids around your table.

I hope you're walking a more peaceful plain. Forgive me
for a life I didn't have, for my ignorance and pain.
I've been well, if you're willing to make certain allowances.

Most of us stumble through mercy—not too different
from the past, though now at least we know His Name.
Our only comfort is that He never forgets ours.

First Fingers

His digits claw a little at the stone, outside
now: the tentative scrabble; one wonders, could Jesus
have touched people at first? Would He recognize a woman?

Could He bring Himself to put four sticks together?
He had to see them again—the fishermen, Peter.
He had to answer people, with this plenty. So,

the first thing He did was to gather wood for a fire.
He wanted to feel it warm the air, the molecules
change. The molecules, the molecules—part of Him was still

far away. Then He thought of His mother, the welcome in her
    laugh.
He remembered her face, how soft it could be. (It would take
Him some time to get around to the rest of us.)

Earth hovered below His hands, off kilter a bit.
This is what He came back for. (His Father sang in the trees.)
Birds became His friends. The sand, in the dawn, now formed

His skin; the lake. A mist, cold air; a fish plopped,
warming water. He noticed the holes in His feet.
Unfinished, He waited, felt sticks settle in heat.

Brothers to the Tomb

The rocks, for their part, never wavered. The steel stretch
of blue sky held up its end—so would the earth;
the heavier end in any case! Trees wavered

as they always have. The heart of the water, too—
each dapple a part of the puzzle. Rocks could have sung,
did, though no one could hear them, their thrumb, raised

an octave or two. And now the sun, again,
had their face as they held the edifice together, their part
in the universe, through physical strength and meditation.

Brothers to the tomb—their own. They hide what is not
easily revealed, perhaps ever: the parallel reality,
past night. They sound, they sound, like that: now the stars,

now lunch on the grass. They are a deeper ache.
They are the heart of God; they weep because
He's sung them open, their hearts now free as birds.

They hold up their end, like those South of America Jesus
statues. At least someone else hears—stone enough
to be true before called to have the final say.

The Kids Next Door: Elijah, Emma, and Asher

Praise Your Easter Name. I want to claim
Your glory here because now's my only chance.
In heaven everything's a given, so it won't count.

I want to do a ridiculous dance, give way,
give way. This is who we are. Can't you see—
there's no secular world! There's no comfort zone!

Our reach comes from the One who cannot be confined
to a gathered sense of "place," a now. The sky
unrolls in shades of pink, orange—so it must

be morning. I'm sure if I go outside the birds
will show. I'm sure the butcher owns a choice of meats.
(Horticulturists have planted flowers along this path!

They must follow beauty's lead, widen our world.)
We get evenings, TV antennae, the smallest of children:
our neighbor's kids. Each with a packed adult

inside, pushing, a bud of frightful energy,
each waiting for his chance, his force. The days are like this.
God cannot be bothered with ends. He's a maker of means.

My Rusted Saab, with Ibsen

Too much of my god stands in my way. I want
to be completely opened, cobbled, to be one of the forgotten.
That way I could set up a shop in Norway, learn

about fish—with less of me than I could imagine.
My books will help define me. (Jesus likes
to live in the little places, under thatch. He loves

the unfinished sentence, the rise in uneven bread.)
I want to be the whole birch forest where He walks.
When people speak to me, I'm tired of letting

my swerve get in the way. I'd have a better
chance were I to live out of a rusted Saab.
I could hang my laundry, pin a line high from the top

of the passenger door. In a kindly neighbor's back yard
in Oslo. (They might have a small swimming pool.)
Chaos would be my boon companion. He, too, rusted.

We travel each day between what is and what
will be forgotten. Jesus sleeps in a karve
with stormy Ibsen. They float alone on silk.

Reading at Grove City
—for Eric

At the Protestant college, I see the truth again:
the closer we get to Jesus, the farther from wrong.
At our best we're a Eucharist of busy hands, like Bach

at the organ, writing the Mass in B minor to try
and secure a Catholic job. Only music matters.
We find the notes that start to make us clear.

It's a joy when you only have one option, when your reach
precisely expresses what you can't grasp: that fleeting
moment when no amendment is needed. We can't

stop there, of course, own the bus. We must move and lose
what we have gathered until that doesn't matter either.
Let the Japanese plums fall and tumble on the grass!

We can read Rexroth, Hitomaro, occasionally pluck
our shamisen as our Western heads bob in the wind.
Jesus is the only note we can play. He's the chord.

He is the book. (He waits for Himself!) This is how
days go when there's no tabernacle, no face on the floor.
Just a two-story open study—a dear friend who's asked.

Laying Your Wet Hands on the Grass

It's the joke that no one gets, the sunrise that comes
before morning—the Truth delicately awaiting Its telling.
Life's just like that, huge answers sitting around,

waiting for the right question, as summer water
waits for the splash of the child. It's our lives as they continue
to unfold, the expression of both origin and sway!

Each just far enough in front of us! It's like we get more
of ourselves, the closer we get to our end. Jesus
has divined it so! We are the glorious syllables

of God, Him speaking in tongues. We're the One we walk on.
It's why we unroll the carpet of our lives for the people
we meet. It's why those 60s Krishna people

gave flowers away for free (for a time) at the airport,
dressed in those counter-cultural jail-colored robes.
Life is always bringing new ideas—like children's hands

chasing water, a swarm of minnows. You don't need to catch
    them,
your hands marvelously cool and dripping once out.
Should you dry them on your pants or lay them on the grass?

The Eternal Problem of Radishes

I've always had mixed feelings about radishes: that pulpy
angry white neighbor inside. It's enough to make
you wonder about its wild Inventor. Whatever

you have planned in life is simply not relevant.
He has storage closets larger than that. (Too many
mops—like my wife—and He's every bit as charming.)

He gives adult lessons, will teach you how to properly
poise teacups. (Of course, he'll also invite a lumberjack
and a life artist.) He'll give you more friends than you

can handle, and then He'll send them away. (We'll hear
grand trees once again, their big green sigh.) It'll be
like running down the street when you were a kid,

the first three days out of school. It'd be like when you
first learned His name, when He walked in and gave you
your life. Most days here are with your family.

There's joy in the kitchen. It's a place for happy pilgrims.
My wife loves to slice them, create a still life salad.
(Those pale white faces: left-over souls in the moonlight.)

Chuck Norris at Minas Tirith
—for my son, who doesn't want Down's Syndrome

It's the language of emerging leaves: the world as it always
is, becoming, maybe until it gets it right.
You know that this could go in any direction,

and probably will. Each leaf will be itself,
intensely, uttering its small language, bobbing
its peculiar saws in the breeze, a backdrop for Jesus,

who comes right out and speaks Himself as if
the earth were just some coat He could discard—
in the peace and texture of stacked firewood. What else

is there for us to do but to help with the chores?
My Down's son vacuums, never seeing what he brings,
a courage that helps me to direct my days.

(He wants to be more.) That's why we sit at our campground,
invent "three-hour" sagas to roar against the chill.
Ponies and Hobbits, we toss the logs—then our foes.

His life is full of disappointments, though he
can embrace the moment as if he knew its name.
The smallest gifts, friend, they still escape us.

The Hats in the Hat Shop

Life is never lived on our terms, nor will
it end so. That is one of the great goods that own
the hat shop of our lives. Easter minds the till.

(There's a big parade outside, so you, a fedora,
suspend all judgment.) We don't get many days
this nice, and you like the sound of the bell on the door

as it opens, the rush of excitement outside—until
the cycle completes itself. Each person brings
in his own half-completed agenda. Many leave

with something, though never with what they thought.
    That's why
they call them days: gracious stop-overs, tinkling,
but firmly held opinions. What are they worth?

They're like the sound and drawer of the cash register.
Of local, momentary interest. We need Jesus to come in.
Till then, enjoy a box of Jujubes,

a kindly sunset. Let our ignorance be pure. We live
in a metaphorical store with a view. Let creation come,
when we'll sit on happy heads, walk high down the street.

Van Gogh's Yellow Retirement House
—with Kerouac

He must grow larger, as our aging bodies wane.
There's a rightness to this passage, though we don't want to
    leave
rose petals of sorrow for people we love. I'd rather

there were presents under a year-round Christmas tree:
Jesus in a party hat. (That would be Easter too—
but from the other side.) Lord, we come,

as always, as paupers. What do we have to offer
beyond those who come behind? (They are the bright stars
on our foreheads, most of third grade, "St. Louie parochial"!)

Caution, though, has been our middle name.
Still, You take us in, forgive us our swagger.
(I lie as often as I speak.) We gather like beggars

on church steps, St. Joseph Labré—days left at the college.
This is how we know our time is worthwhile—our old faces
decline. Each opportunity passes slowly, a noisy

coupling: trains braking in the night. Van Gogh would've felt
at home here: his ear in an Easter basket! Jesus
gather us listening, flowers for Your yellow house.

The Most Unlikely People

Praise God for the light that brings these days, for the flagstone
that keeps them. The next life has always been available,
the reason for this one. The barrel in which we fish.

Let the students swim upstream; let my children cut
their teeth on the world's lies. Let freedom be
their middle name. They are an Easter people;

let them cry out to the stars, the poles. They will know
the incomplete reach of their children's toys, each one,
a heavenly intervention. St. John Paul II

was like that. I saw him once in a movie pick up
some cheese that had fallen on the floor. He wiped it off,
then ate it as he talked to the other actor. I want

to be like that: an answer of one. I want
to go about my business, calm as a good Muenster.
He came to me once, as warm as he must've been

when he had the job he was made for. (He liked me—my
    work!)
As ready to help as Faustina. Who would have thought that?
God always hangs out with the most unlikely people.

Whistling like a Bird

"Poetry is contemplation," Merton tells us.
It's an egg on a windowsill, or the baseball cards you had
as a child—that kid who was your friend. The presence

of God haunted our childhoods. He whistled down our street,
collected blackberries in the woods with us. He was
my baseball dream, me pounding my glove on my bed,

as I prayed that the rain would stop: the stick in my uniform
letters—from the sweaty insides. He followed me down
the years, usually in the background. (This process is never lost

on anyone.) We knew his sorrow, even as we came into
our own: no fulfillment here; no dream could ever
be large enough. Those Easters promised what they

would never deliver. Beer and poetry helped.
For their time. They allowed me a run to play things out.
(College did much the same.) It was part of the arc,

like the one I caught in Mott's biography, Jesus
allowing Merton his epic life. Mine includes
an ability to amuse my grandson by whistling like a bird.

Better the Patch Job
—down a retreat wood-path

Will I live to see the better man, the unselfish
one, the one who forgets his imagined due?
The world would be utterly changed—or almost. It would be

a place my body could more completely recognize.
The shops would be small, the coins, all new. Lots of
other people would speak out loud to themselves, walking

down Mister Rodgers Avenue. There would be a small-ish
statue, a tribute! I will know each of my neighbors,
all the way down the street. Birds will invent

new tunes. I will learn to skeet shoot. (So you can see
the problem that would arise: our imaginations, no matter
how good, would pale. Violence would follow.) Besides,

who has time to wait for that guy who would only annoy you?
Better the patch job. Here quandary can console. In a way,
we're already men for others, somewhere, offering

ourselves in our limited way for the greater good.
The trick is to notice what matters: a coolness in the air,
the familiar tree-path on a sunless jacket of a day.

Jesuit Retreat Woods, Walking

Easter stretches, like the back of our necks when our work
moves past our efforts. Our joy doesn't last. Or what
we remember of it—that yesterday late morning place

where leaves shone sun-bright on the younger and farther,
much taller trees: different greens at different depths—
holy hands, moving behind each other in the breezes.

God's canvas, a place to remember friends, alive
or not. And Jesus, heaven, a dispensation.
Our Lady may leave you flowers. A few saints line up.

Joy reoccurs, what it feels like here when the sun
bears a bright blue shield, mottling the foliage
inside you. It doesn't matter how many trees crashed

last night in the rain. Or that a buck, young, stands
in the same trace of path near the back fence
at both ten and two o'clock; several does,

at the earlier hour, on the other side. (On a retreat
every symbol matters!) Perhaps it's who we are,
in one need or another. This will always be our plight.

The Double Speech of God
—Panhandle Walking Trail, Weirton

Easter sings, like Beethoven, or the smooth slope
of a mushroom's cap, its ventilation system, the slits
underneath. She is the open mouth of the Lord.

She drifts like small sticks on the river. Another day
has come! Larger than the one before. Who
could contain it? I wish my childhood friends could hear

these waters. On the wooden bench which faces the slips:
the folds, the white. Perhaps they have. There's no joy
anywhere else. We can hear it, these late spring days.

The whole of creation cries: "You have helped make me so."
We are, together, the newest thing: Jesus-
God and me. The river chases itself,

adores what holds it, running. The cold distance I sometimes
feel does not matter. That is temporary.
So we walk here together, wait to complete the play

that accomplishes itself. What You have given has always
just started. My hand raises in the form that forms it.
It's a kind of holy stutter, the double speech of God.

Mondrian's Foot

The heart of Jesus is like Matisse's cutouts,
or the florescent café light that buzzes in the doorway.
(An artist inside has become a clotted shoe brush!)

We can't understand a lampstand. This frees us, friend,
to express our varied opinions, to give them numbers.
We'll become a New York neighborhood of little horns,

moving Mondrians, the yellow and red rectangles.
(Or are they houses that move along his tracks?)
We might learn to talk in a series of Catholic beeps.

Jesus would be good with that, a Clint Eastwood cigar
out of His second mouth. (You may not have
His address—a short pony for the kick and chase.)

How could you possibility want anything here? Even
were you to range, settle into New Mexico, your wisdom
would fail you. No, we need the flower and half

its stem! We need to finish in another world.
We need to meet flat, one-eyed friends, fish-mouthed,
each blinking in surprise, inside a blue café.

Dinner with Bob Dylan

I ate my chocolate bunny, the other ear
in the grass. (A gladness seemed to pervade the neighborhood!
Doors started to open as strawberry plants now tossed

their white heads this way then that, losing petals.)
We watched the ROLLING THUNDER, my wife and me.
Were orthodox Catholics there, we wonder? Why not?

We were under-represented. I demand a recount!
All the Catholics I know are off making modern art,
wire and neon plaster sculpture. Or they've opened

Our Lady of Guadalupe Pizza Shops,
have stopped caring about what the world is up to.
Garabandal is their spiritual home. America is not

God to them, or the way to get there. She is humble
stone, a path that needs to be worn down.
How else could Jesus come to flower, crack open

the walls of the dead? Here is always the place, the cobb
that feeds us. We send up our big-tire pick-ups, our gardens,
in a neighborhood filled with rednecks, incompleted Jews.

"To the Moon, Alice"
—the early sixties by Flannery O'Connor

Jesus, You're next of kin to the lost, where sorrow
follows like the delayed "to the moon" of a battered boy,
the ketchup he used: America's first spaceship. Wisdom

has to widen us. We're too knowledgeable to lift a hand
in time, to own who we are. Everything must be
revealed. Art Carney save us. (Our Sheppard must

do so, collect our first orbit!) So thank You, Jesus,
for my sins. They make me see myself, what I am
without (or with) you. They level. May they carry my fiction

down my hobbling days. I don't want Your joy. That
comes later in the story. I want chaw at a general store.
(I'm every clown I've ever met.) In darkness

is light. We are all that motherless child. Wake us.
Give us a soldier's matching limp while You're at it—
please, a polio shoe like my father wore.

These stories aren't imagined. They're an us that keeps
    happening;
they're a criminal welcome, down a long corridor. May we
    never
lose our troubles—or the architecture that will help us live
    them.

Two Brothers, Widening my Retreat

> —I can't eat the potatoes for dinner
>   and so take a drive to my brother's house;
>   another is, surprisingly, there as well.

It's easy to forget who we are, maybe because
we drift so far from home, rewriting star charts,
petting new dogs. We want more. Let me offer

desert amends: an evening tambourine, beat
it slowly against my palm on a western plateau.
Let me frame the proceedings. Or better, let my brothers.

I met them—surprisingly—today, away from here,
both part, my Director says, of a widened retreat:
one, a maverick, the other, perhaps, too giving,

both twisted up—I see just now—how each lives
the only life their baggage could allow; each considered
excess, a precise way to rise above,

to give salvific assent to our father, that marvelous
and brutalizing stamp which made us. They offer imitation,
compensation. They're like the evening primrose in the desert,

covering it in paper. They hold life together—
which is their glory. They are him, made whole; completing
our family, those postwar projects, those neighbor-less hoods.

A Danxia Landform Fiction
—for Xuefei Yang, YouTube

Whose brushes made that desert sing? And how detached
she must have felt at night when the colors disappeared!
Easter, friends, fades. Someone graffities the rolled stone,

or buys a Bible, commentaries, at a convenient store.
Everything that is good becomes something less. And then,
what are we left with? Day-old take-out, late summer

grass, lighter in color, a ritual we needed
to have. (She wanted jewels on the straps of her gown;
the Party—a relaxed world order, older than memory.)

But neither could evoke it long enough to make a difference.
What was there to be grateful for? That, she knew.
Music had made her—not whole—but real. She had started

out thinking her guitar was a boat she could sail over
startled seas, that those white doors would open.
But in the end, she could only leave them the stage,

with parts of themselves. And they certainly didn't mind that.
God was in all of it, was all of it. That is why
she does this, can drink her tea alone in the afternoons.

The Days are the Thanks We Give

Easter is where we grow. Our plantings won't make
BETTER HOMES AND GARDENS, but Jesus honks
when the green starts talking. I can also run beside

my mad grandson's little bike in the alley, my son
at the opposite flank, closer, helping with the handlebars,
keep enough second banana comic distance,

flapping, crowing, not allowing my choices to interrupt
the flow. Everything gets lost to the joy, the way
it should be. I am like leaves or old motor oil.

Like the rocks that rim the garden, I will eventually sink.
No one, thankfully, will care very much. Any splash
I make will register on the other, heavenly side.

Will I wish I'd done better? Sure. But we all wish that now.
So why complain? The soup's good, and I talked to a nice
      student
after class today. (My wife met an old art framer.)

Sometimes the two of us sit together at night
on the couch, watch art on TV, or walk the dog.
The days are the thanks we give, the wave across the street.

Their Failures, like Money to Me
—last morning of retreat

Jesus, what's here? Pan pipes, a sunny afternoon?
The cool promise of heaven? The humus of my life?
It's lonely and cold, where the portions get smaller—if we're
    blessed.

No one of any importance will meet us on the roads
out of here. We won't care! The wet asphalt will recommend
itself. It's Jesus, the dark, which will give it meaning.

We're like the fingers on Your left hand, Lord, a rise
in birds and later temperature; so many changes,
kind of like how heaven will be when it comes. Jesus,

Easter is the call that invents us, the towering city.
Who could move and not find succor? Today will be
another canvas, Your absent vote. Like the e-mail

I just got from my wife! She and our two adult kids,
both other-abled, picking strawberries in my absence.
I can picture them, counties away, struggling to lift

that twist-tied net! It would be nice to be there, share jokes,
staining my fingers with my life, my home place
in the dirt. Their failures will be like money to me.

That Party Under the Hill

Saints are quiet as a night lake, when the only
sound you hear is the breeze that rocks your boat,
the splash of your oars. That's the startling point. The Spirit

that animates is never hidden. It exists in the love
between old spouses, in surfaces like polished wood.
And how attentive the Church is in finding her hidden

friends. We can try to move that way today;
we can embrace the forgotten. Easter glistens
there on water "across the clear flat glass

before sunrise." Each holy voice absorbs, diffuses
life. They're an extension, not a definition, a musical
scale in nature. They're the only Jesus there is:

St. Thérèse in the woodpile. And you know with what vigor
    she'd chop;
just another piston in the rough engine of heaven—
our woods. There may be dark seas ahead. Death

will be required—that party under the hill,
with dark hoods, bock beer. Strangers will hold hands
for the first time; we won't need anybody's name.

Eostre, Odes, and the Worst Line in English Poetry

We need to feel the thorns of life, to bleed;
we need to feel rivers rive our veins.
How else could we be sure that we are alive?

Jesus owns it all, gives the present,
even as it falls apart: death's blackened hectic
leaves. Each is a point of origin in a world that can't

complete itself. Our hair riots in every wind!
Name things quickly, friend; they die—the bitter
part of blackest berries! We need to count

our losses—the things we've depended upon. Each
of us, on a hill, with our heroic proportions.
Yes, Jesus, yes. The years leave us only this:

You're the Wind, driving each revelation, apostasy.
Each uttered word speaks You, brands us, Bede's
Eostre. (Our ancient bodies are pagan to the core.)

They know the us that's here is earth, that we eat
to die. We shock the trees, run dirt tails—praising
Your darkest name, arguing in dervishes of leaves.

Holy Dirt and Saturn
—Chimayo, New Mexico

The packed dirt writes its name beyond the sky;
the birds, too, come back to eclipse their song.
They insist upon some farther back—Saturn, the deep

space that no one was around to hear; or the first
human hair they found floating on water. Native Americans
have their tales, always somehow defining You

with You, like a bald eagle—its flight too clean
for metaphor. You cover these mountains, vales, have never
heard a name You didn't like. The physical is precisely

You. Like finely etched glass, or Mormons, in their bonnets,
coming over the Utah rise. They have wives enough
and children to recommend them. And you can always count

on their smiles. So what if so much of their theology
is sails in the wind. Everyone has burdens. Whole Protestant
nations have their backs. Every day there's a table laid out

for no clear reason: woven Navajo blankets;
that holy, healing dirt you can buy at Chimayo.
Those crutches indict us, help us to find our seats.

Late Spring Drive: "Spinning" with Jude
—"There is a Mountain"

God never hurries through time. You can see that in
the trees, on gravel roads. More green arrives
every day. The rains ease, the breath of God

finds you up a rural rise, as the sun begins
to set, just what's left of the storm. The world is too beautiful
for words in southeastern Ohio, my son snoozing

in his seat. Our lives are like this, too, we can only
hope: changing imperceptibly toward the good.
Either way, it's the beauty which sustains us.

We find ways to see it as we answer its call—
the first bird I just heard, writing, in the dark early morning.
(Maybe all this has something to do with Donovan, who

I've been googling for some reason.) There is a gentleness
Jesus brings when you get to yourself. Those moments
don't happen often enough, "caterpillar." We "shed"

our "skin," each just as unfashionable as the previous take.
That's where peace lies, always outside the times,
on a road no one else (but you and your son) can take.

Under the Flower of Night

The world moves above us, with its kings, its sewer systems.
We won't hear the last drop of hot oil hit
the pan before the kingdom comes. (May we miss most of that.)

Our small circles have their advantages; hipness wanes,
or at least limps badly—enough to draw no glance.
May our laughter never extend beyond this small room,

its array of holy candles. Pope Francis will be here
with the saints, their quiet voices and maybe a vase
of flowers. In the meantime, we have our sins and beads

to count, our troublesome days. Our merits—a struggling
band of malcontents. He must move our tents into Galilee,
the shops, wells, the Jezreel palms; always

with those scribes, guardians at the local holy gates.
Teach us to fish, to mend our quiet nets.
We'll go back to the sea, catch more species than

we'll know what to do with. I will find my father's house,
make friends with the earth, the sea again, its sky.
Things always came together under the flower of night.

Humility is a Coat that doesn't Fit

The slow sway of Japanese irises, their movement
is toward summer. Like God, whose scope is so large—
what else could we expect? Even when we don't

feel it, we carry out His demands—our residual part.
Jesus, King-Lord, let our mouths speak one syllable:
mercy. Let the rocks cry out, "The donkeyed One

is still passing!" Our palms do not betray us.
We are His though we can't move past ourselves. Humility
is a coat that doesn't fit, every day of our lives.

This becomes increasingly so as time passes:
old ones walk slower, in the Russia of Dostoevsky,
today. Our bodies balk, talk back. They're in

slow fall toward the earth. (But they'll have to wait!)
Being slow helps them to see, to endure what must
be known. Our King is laying the past to rest.

The old can hear what's coming in migratory birds.
Their hands, praying along, are like a clamor
rising among reeds, very early some other morning.

Pig Take
—after Beatrix Potter

All glory is Yours. There isn't any left to go
around. That would be like hanging a necklace on a pig,
charming though the porker might be. (Oh, she'd be a sight

amongst her fellows, a jaunt; light on her feet.
And being of impressive girth, she might be granted
the queen's walk; though at the end of that town, she'd still

look porcine, slumbering alone with her short snorts.)
So it is for everyone; we sashay when we get the call,
elected after too long a wait: to the hall of shame—

to the front of the lunch line. It's not that we're unworthy;
it's just that we get the context wrong. Why shouldn't
a pig enjoy herself, after all? There's fun

for all at the trough, rooting along the fence—
because there's always a pecking order, isn't there?
Along walls, through skinny passages. In the end she lives here,

under piggy constellations, the grunting of night or too early
a sun. (It's not a good look, being so large
and caught squinting—skirts too short for a lady.)

When Spring is Large Enough

The vast days can be friends, varied and green.
Driving over flat land, the blue and those fat
white and stiffly flat-bottomed greyish clouds—

the remains of winter—take over. (The blue is new
after rains.) Nature is a call from home on days
like this: a bit too cold for comfort, perhaps,

but a heavenly directive: impermanence. These days are like
    shells
on a beach, the trace of shine up their cool ridges,
the ordinary miracles we can never take for granted,

or for long. We come outside here and something larger
takes over. What response could be adequate? Quiet, in a car,
my son now sleeping beside me, his music on the radio.

There's a riot in these changes: what will have Itself.
It takes what you are and remakes you, delivers you
from fiction, your small scrap of reality. Every day

chooses to do this, in the kitchen, at the table; your say
is small enough to count, though not for much.
This is why you take a stick when you go for a hike.

The Rockets' Glare
—August, 2021

Easter seasons; it scorches the land between Lebanon
and Palestine. His tomb was just the first to open.
(It obliterated the distance between this world and the next.)

You want prophecy? Find the line that runs down the middle
of your violent heart. Every tomb is yesterday's news.
(Man created rockets and found them good!)

Jesus waits to realize Himself in the flesh of this world.
It was what He was born for. (His days of squatting by the
    shore,
cupping up guppies are nearly gone, my friend.)

Our place in this is the same as it's always been.
He is the water. We are the fish. We fall
in its sun-flaked falling, rise as You breathe us again.

The tv has never defined us. That is a tale told
by an idiot. So too, big money which tries so hard
to bag and seal these days. In the end, it's the King

who walks. We gladly fold with him, making
our necessary noises: bleats, pasturing our lives.
That's one reason why our voices never echo that far.

Chopin's Nocturne Op. 9 No. 2

The good doesn't overwhelm; we have our lives to live.
Days happen slowly, we wait for their meanings to unfold.
Water lilies come to mind, Monet's, at night,

when the art museum's lights are low. Just me
or you in there, making our unguided rounds.
We can stay for as long as we'd like. And today, on retreat,

it rains all day, softly. My books are gathered
on the desk. I'm scheduled to see my Director soon.
Everything happens for reasons beyond us, even weather!

Chopin's music is about that—beaded windows.
It's about the dance one has to make alone.
There's no hurrying as we wait: empty days

and how we fill them. Our acts still don't define us:
my chair moves, this desk does not. We cannot
hear the order, the bigger music—the hands

of Jesus assuming our own. We seldom see this
as we create our night flowers, a young Chopin
in 1832: his piano hears us—in the rain!

The Cracks of Dawn (for Harry Clarke)

Praise You for this day that's always coming—apart,
the cracking dawn. Like any plans, in my hands;
but the constructed roseate mosaic that follows should please.

(We need these.) For God's part, He doesn't seem to mind.
He's ready to go with what He's got. It's like when we turn
to face another human—we do what we can.

Thank You, Jesus, for our persistent clumsiness,
for the provisional government. It's a province we can work in,
a land where children can thrive. (We can't expect much.)

Still, the more or less of it satisfies in some way.
Our King knows us. And if we keep getting up,
we're going in the right direction. We're Ireland, broken:

Harry Clarke, his Geneva window (in Miami),
those glistening blues: we're an unconscious firefly, a flue
we live by, share, a molten turn, who we

will be! (We give light to the stars.) The deep follows,
unshaken, but changed as if his blues alone
were behind its making! (The best dances happen at night.)

Ascension and Return

Is this why we always look up, to see the sky change
again? We want something beyond red, lining pink,
the orange; we want something beyond a sun setting

after itself. We want the last cupped egg
to crack beneath His earnest spoon. We want
the world to complete Itself. The next sky, too,

will be blue. (Like that huge yellow turtle I found by the side
of the road, a living Native American myth,
we'll take back the earth.) My soul, my neighborhood,

these things escape me, as I haul my clothes to the cleaners.
The steam endures as I carry them back to the car.
Its emissions make me clean, at least for a while.

Still, it's the sky we come for. Not the empty table,
the one upon which I feast. I live too far
below, among the dogs and horses, the rail

fences which, thankfully, defeat me. Every good here has got
to come to an end. That's our only way home:
when palest stars come out in the middle of the day.

When Mr. Weir, the Steel Magnate, Stuck Up a Coach
—Weirton, WV

The new is for suckers. And the old, it's always a nice
visit—the smell of everything at grandma's house:
green pillow mints, the flat-ironed white tablecloth.

A tradition without both is dead: "The Church at Auvers,"
doorless, and the candle dark within. The heart
needs room to make its world. That's why Vincent and Francis

walk together in heaven, each wants to hear the other's
song. "He who is free is free indeed," Jesus says,
His beret a-tilt, as he chooses a new walking stick.

My Lord, let the small leaves fall down upon us
when we visit the city park across the river.
Linda will bring her pens, her pad; she'll be like

that nursery worker we met yesterday. He recounted
history: the intransigent Carnegie bankers in Pittsburgh—
the immigrants hired by Mr. Weir to stick up

a coach; him spending steel money for years,
paying them back. "God is wild," says Gerald Stern,
as King David does a dance, as we plant local seeds.

Chelsea Morning (or Joni Mitchell's Cane)

I've never been to Kiev, nor to Caminito
in Buenos Aires. And I don't have an earring chime,
or stilts, or a six-foot face mask to walk behind—

though I did once have a student named Mahto Fast Horse.
The point is, beautiful mornings tell us how much
we must leave behind. This would include all that wonderful

South American street art. Which is too bad;
it would have been lovely to have lunch there with my wife.
Had we that chance, we would have found our own sights.

Meeting locals would feel like today: May 20th
is new every year. My wife is out back this morning,
finding new ways to prop up the hose, so she

can water strawberries as she strews new pots, plants.
My Downs' son Jude has officially requested fun.
But that must wait until I finish this draft.

My wife and I are older now, like the sun
this morning, still early in its rise. We might miss it one day.
The thing is, what's new is old—the converse too!

I Want Your Breath

I want Your breath—near my head. I want to smell
the sea of Galilee, to hear the vibration in Your voice.
I want to be overwhelmed by the God of You.

You are love Itself, a code that has to crack us,
a fence along a beach I cannot hop.
They say You speak to the heart, but I want more

than that. I want completion, now, I want
to be how I am known. My soul was made
for this. When will You give the rest? When will

You make me You? Don't get me wrong. This is no
rock pile. You come out in flowers, always petalling,
light rain dripping from their woven colors, fabric.

Perhaps that's all I can bear: beauty. (A car
beeps softly outside this morning.) But tell me, how
can I be prepared for my end if I don't cross over?

I know. I'm not John of the Cross. What he endured
is beyond me. I have milk money in my pocket.
I'll fashion stranger, longer routes to school.

CPSIA information can be obtained
at www.ICGtesting.com
Printed in the USA
BVHW031626140422
634019BV00001BA/6